FUGITIVE SHADOWS

By

Dr. Muhammad Rafique Farooqi

COPYRIGHT @ FUGITIVE SHADOWS
By Dr. Muhammad Rafique Farooqi

ISBN:
Hardbound-978-621-470-247-3
MOBI/KINDLE-978-621-470-248-0
Softbound/Paperback-978-621-470-249-7

Published by:
Poetry Planet Book Publishing House
Rosario, Pozorrubio, Pangasinan, Philippines
Contact Number: 09554960094
Email: maritesritumalta@gmail.com

DEDICATION

My poetry book is dedicated to my father, who always loved books and made a collection of about 2000 books at home for the family.

PREFACE

I began writing poetry in 2005 when words gave me precious hope and my mind could comprehend with grace enhancing my spirit to faith. This glorified my poetic enlightenment and more inspiration to the existence, guiding me that success is always there. Felt a miraculous presence of gladness leading me to the right path, steering my way to trust and dignified bliss of reassurance to reach my destination. I felt my dreams are vibrant like fire filling in my soul with the purest prudence. My poetry is uplifting for the dejected and crestfallen and for the person fighting to come out of scalding life. As the sadness is concealed by man, it hurts the heavy hearts. But clouds make rain when they become heavy. Every day with new hope. Life is a beautiful gift of God, remember always this and go ahead with hope for better.

Dr.Muhammad Rafique Farooqi
Author

TABLE OF CONTENTS

EVERGREEN

When I feel different,

sometimes,

Grudges grunt,

Over spics of anger,

debris of hate swells to degenerate,

Into sparks of elusive traits,

whereas I spare,

My actions,

To seed peaceful emotions,

calling a spade a space,

And wrong a wrong, sky and earth,

appear kind,

when I face with my open eyes,

you can see,

with all this, rains and winds,

keep green alive. and evergreen.

LET US JOIN

just come,
and color my sleep,
with dreams,
sun rays,
and laser beams,
and never shatter,
whatever may be matter.
anyway
you are sweet,
like a heartbeat,
and stay with me,
in a dreamy island,
with breezes,
and sunflowers,
for long-lasting,
hours,
this blue sky, this blue sea,
is ours, these clouds,
these rains,
joys,
happiness,
all types of pain,
our success,
vain,
any strain,
any good,
or bad weather will be taken,
together

MUTATION

Blood is bitter nor sweet,

not even sour,

it seems a taste of death,

blended with ashes and dust,

innocents slain with pains,

who is to stop feuds,

fires grow in grasses,

and winds rush through

windows when newborn screams for life,

sun blazes the sands,

peace glitters like a mirage,

man mutates into a monster,

when life is bitter than death.

THE NEXT DAY

Glitters of snow linger in eyes,

like a taste of a promised bliss,

a hangover of conscious,

in the chill of night,

lost in mists of dismay,

and a shiver of hands,

catching the tremors,

when a spark of fire dreamed in mind,

and face of winds,

refused by a mirror,

While rose petals,

dropping like tears,

and numbed bare feet,

weary and lost,

the journey,

begins with a heart of defeat,

there is some room,

upon the top of the hill,

as I lock the door,

waiting for the next day.

THE VOYAGE

Just the day, comes,

with an iron will,

the way to conquer the passions,

standing strong for the will,

droned by halfhearted gestures,

and sick blood,

heated to warm,

inhabiting the frozen hope,

Clenched jaw,

over the aggressions,

a defeated wish,

to surrender, famous faces,

staring sky, the voyage,

with the design of numbness,

against the howling winds,

and in deep waters.

TOURNAMENTS

I dream I promise,
I break up,
I shatter,
like unstable,
moments,
in life,
countless,
in occasions,
but,
I still wonder,
over,
my internal distortions,
viable,
noises raised up to the neck,
occasional severity,
in behavior disorder,
and shutdown,
of all random priorities,
to pay breaths as ransom,
to life,
with fetters over the body,
emptying my lungs,
with labored exhale,
how you can believe when lies are,
ornaments of face,
and swamps of sins,
to drag me in,
you are generous,

to offer me,
your hand,
in epic moments,
with the traction of my arm,
but gravity,
increasing my weight,
to infinity,
death comes,
with light speed,
Einstein writes,

EMC2

on my forehead,

Alexander conquers my will,

Aristotle confuses,

the situation,

whatever,

it may be,

hidden,

and dormant,

t ornaments,

erupting from the soil.

under my feet

WARS

I drift down,
when I listen to utterances,
reverberating in my mind,
these are not melodies,
but dances of hunger and sickness,
over the broken crusts of earth,
In downtowns on real grounds.
where sky burns and ashes,
soar in hurricane winds.
where breeze does not mean,
and fires of war rain with blood,
and clouds of dark smokes,
and cannon rumbles shake the hearts,
Where life is deeper than graves,
and death may give it up,
embracing the tragic,
Can man find himself?
with wavering wisdom,
gripping necks with shaking hands,
with suffered tolerance,
In a house of fantasies.
with open eyes,
and buried dreams,

WITHERING WHISPERS

Memories of pain,

still droning on,

to dampen the exuberance,

of my faith in you,

raging on my brittle defeats,

you run over my silent desires,

to celebrate,

your day of vicarious victory,

and our vested tryst,

limping along,

desperate moments,

fading into oblivion,

and as I know,

you're not as vile,

as I thought.

FIRE OF TURMOILS

Watching the events,

from a distance,

having a thin slice of glimpse,

accolade may be,

matter of pride,

or something at bigger stakes,

denouncing a dissident on turmoil,

wrapped crush on breaths,

repentance over past sins,

partially sensible,

motivated by anger and love,

inscrutable to know the real,

bitterly tasted with frenzied joy,

worsened by fascination,

we get from the people,

we can't understand.

NO WAY TO LIVE

When everything was at stake
I was unable to hold on to my dreams
For the primitive desire
That still lingers on
The fossils of primates
Though that life is a forgotten tale
With the passing of time
I will never abandon my sovereign traits

As I stay in a closet
With no noise and no voice
And no step will be getting closer
To the door
Just when I stare at the roof
I see no sky
which is kind enough
To keep me as uttered voice
In the silence of deafness

Suffer the Cruelties of the time
Waiting for the end of the days
Prone to the judgment
Reaved on settlement
Where no one fits to survive
No one claims to yonder through
The luxuries of life

Like the dire wolves
It is bitter to be remembered
A forgotten way of the desert
Straying and waiting for promises
Longing for inborn sovereignty
Paralyzed by inaction
Where defining moments can be mortifying
From the self-inflicted suffering
With the privilege of necrosis
And ongoing decay.

RAGE OF HONOUR

Rumble of sparkling,
awaking the peace hating,
monster minded,
licking the victory songs,
written on walls of history,
with ancient spells,
roaring in the dark caves,
back for hunting,
the heads of ages,
again unsheathing their swords,
of ill design.

mothers crying for newborns,
and the sun was eaten by the eclipse,
and the blood of civil, quenching the thirst of evil,
and the suicidal bombers invading the streets,
with virulent aims,

poisoning the ears,
with their outcasted lies.
this invisible enemy,
carcinogen to life,
hiding in the laps of civilization
Wanting to terminate,
The days and nights,
To smokes of darkness.

RIGHT BUT LATE

Strains stretching,

my neurotic spells,

and hate rendering,

whatsoever,

the humour burning to the miser,

staring walls with the design of ill.

Glottis to strangulate,

with hopeless utter,

and crying feeble to hoarse

Like a bird to disappear on the horizon and desire

longed to finish,

like candle thread,

another desert stands to cross along,

and feet to blister with hot sand,

a storm is to blow his whistles,

like the hiss of a snake,

and mine struggles are right but late

UNUSUAL STRESSES

I wanted to see you,
In dreams,
and always,
It lingers,
Like mists,
and smokes,
In spaces,
before my visions,
but in realities people,
find empty mosaics,
filled with airs,
rather beautiful fluids,
Like wines of dreams,
so in a jiffy,
I saw you, In a crowd,
like a cloud,
below a hot sun,
I felt everything drifting,
in my eyes,
I found myself,
alone,
and nothing,
alive around me,
I walked a journey,
on a barren road of life,
and smokes became still,
before my eyes,

WAITING EYES

My waiting eyes,
chilled in clouds,
wandering above the,
frozen peaks of the mountains.,
where darkness at night,
and brightness of snow at day blinds me,
and fears of frostbite,
blown whistles of furious winds,
are to push me to drift in death valley,
why I want to know your presence,
close to my mind,
where the warmth of life,
is with survival,
my limbs are grabbed by white bears,
and they want me,
to drag in their caves,
and these bears are happy,
to find some taste of red blood,
I want finally to know reality,
do you love,
to see me at this particular moment,
when I am to find asylum in the heavens.

COOL WITH WORDS

Stars moon

Sun and sky,

we love to find,

and relate our pain or joy,

and fluttering winds,

clouds and birds,

our murmuring lips,

singing words,

and dancing rainbows

with love when grows,

sunshine and rains,

soothing our body pains,

breeze and green grasses,

and flowers when tossed,

standing trees and hills,

warm weathers and cool rills

giving hopes against fears,

giving life and wiping tears,

UNREAL AND REAL

The past is something,

you lost,

and becoming last of the last,

and future is the weather forecast,

the paradise is distant,

dream, walking empty hands,

a sketch made on the sands,

When we see by closing eyes,

Our vision dies,

Placing the universe on the temporal measure,

one page of life we tear,

better to do, what you want,

and leave what you don't want.

YOUR SMILES

Your smiles,

give me feathers,

my wings flutter to soar,

and your smiles shine like a rainbow,

growing after pleasant rains.

I am feeling your breaths,

inhaling heavenly musks,

I am sinking in your smiles,

deep blue, and clear waters,

and fresh roses with dew,

your smiles make me know.

how my vigours grow.

GOLDEN DREAM

milestones embedded,

in dreams,

and journey of nights,

is something different,

in lights and sounds,

tribals dancing on,

the roadside,

with golden bowls in hands,

fireflies moving like stars,

the road ended in the,

river and gold water,

running down,

and crystal boat approaching me,

I am to cross the river,

before the lights and,

sounds are over,

HOMELESS LOVE

Thirst is never quenched,

by a distant vision of the water,

It burns like a desire,

Consumed, and contracted,

With blazing of time,

You may trim the clay of hopes,

from outcast of ambitions,

and days to return empty-handed and worn.,

making fallen leaves your,

Only ornament,

Fate is. a street boy,

crying over a broken toy,

Your silence,

meant for confession,

unwanted sins,

dragging weary feet,

on the bend of the street,

Just with homeless and,

wayward love.

SELF REHABILITATION

Over with dilapidated,

outcast of past,

needless to regret,

over-sentimental erosion,

deplorable skeletal wreaks,

amendable with back steps,

Cognizant of perceptible,

hands of kindliness,

and hopeful disposition.

This day is nothing,

like others,

the glide of soaring wings,

against the winds,

Over the sea waters,

a breakthrough,

is needed just,

with passage of time.

OF OFFENCE

on one day or the other,

some occult desire,

blinding my soul,

with fall of my dignity,

over the betrayal of breaths,

when immortal worth dueled,

in sovereignty,

looking beyond ethics is bleeding in tears, yes,

insane desire hangs unfinished,

but what breeds, in my chest,

someone knows the flame,

hurting my tissues,

but the edge of offense,

is more than I can see.

RAT ON THE MOON

[t is wild chilled outside,

through a foggy window,

I can see still,

snow to yonder through,

frozen white oaks,

glittering in the moonlight,

and with the silence of the night,

and fragile crystallized love,

and grey spotlight on my tail,

touching down, silk fur,

my pink lips and, delicate nose tip,

and small white ivory teeth,

and sharp hunting,

claw, winged chariot coming,

to me in glories,

me for the warmth of journey to,

brightened moon,

and looked so beautiful,

bright and blue-chip green,

I never ever seen,

and moon soft and plumped,

a white mouse with a pink tail,

jumping high amazing delight,

I was also to jump higher, feeling light,

little resisting baby,

drifting gently from my throat.

LIFE

Keeping with precarious existence,

life moves with,

inertial steps, to do a little,

When soil is soaked with tears,

weekend breaths smelling foul,

steep wall standing ahead,

Opaque dream overnight,

thunderstorm roaring aloud,

One desire of hunting beast,

blowing brute in the ears,

Paining corns on feet,

and journey. make me tired

MOON AND STAR

Moon and star, are closer,

Is the ocean,

Turbulent,

Is the moon pulling sea waves,

I hope so,

Weathers are predators,

Breaking the silence,

Waves are pouring,

Gems and stones,

Out of the sea,

Wait for the morning,

And singing breeze

NIGHT WALK

The day went with tranquilities,
The night is to quite chirps of birds,
Longing shadows,
To rule the events,
Erupting tears from depths,
Over the blood from veins,
Hope is pushed to walls,
The big bray of time,
Shaking the tides of moments,
who is to take care of,
Newborn moon,
Evils grow from swamps,
Of ugly greed.
This brawl of a few hours,
Knocks out the revenge,
And makes to think the minds,
By skipping wilfully,
and closing both eyes,
Entering the next day,
With both feet.

ONE BY ONE

To stray like unskilled, and unfortunate,

with futile gestures and abortive aims,

It is not always,

To lose every time,

When everyone comes,

barefoot and empty-handed,

who knows the written fortune,

and shining lucks, and to live

with the uneven endeavor to survive,

and ruling perils and insomniac eyes,

uncertain and wrecked, broken dreams,

and nightmares, ruining everyone, one by one.

SILENCE AND LOVE

On the silence,
grown on your side,
a fire that drags,
in my mind,
I drift in, when you call me,
Counting the flow,
Of river of love,
your eyes flash,
In the color of wine when musks linger,
behind you,
I wander like,
a bird with wings,
roses vanish to know,
the Lights,
on the lips of morning rise,
glow shining on your cheeks,
smile ripples,
from the warmth of dimples,
life begins within my heart,
I close my eyes,
to catch this dream,
and inhale a breeze of love.

STALKERS

Growing with silence,

unwelcomed,

and think stunningly,

in crowed of life,

stear, with own,

deeper than the skin,

haunting dreams,

and nightmares,

overwhelming treacherous,

an existence which follows,

Stepped down,

Sounds of steps,

Sneezing over daffodils,

Climbing the steep walls.

WHEN I FEEL ALONE

Tonight I will forget my pains,
As snow is piled up all around,
and glittering in low moonlight,
Mists on windows of my house,
brought some memories biting my mind.
when a deer collided head-on,
With my car,
and forgot to cry in despair
losing vitals in minutes,
And I feel night breathing in silence,
I am with loneliness,
and shadows of dreams,
Yellow light is seen from a distant house,
Awakening pain of my sore eyes,
when I suffer from my sleep,
spending sound of the clock,
and my heartbeats,
overlapping the pin-drop silence,
I inhale a deep breath,
find a book under my pillow,
with the title of a cute kid,
reading the 1st page,
Sleep lures me to tranquilize,
and the day comes during the time,
I am ready to move,
Good morning,
My soul.

WHERE TO GO

Beware of his evils,

when doing good to someone,

and close this chapter,

When it is, fairly done,

The river when flows,

It knows,

Where the flow goes,

Day or night,

It does not matter,

To remain,

tolerant and steady,

And to end,

In endless,

That matters.

SILLY DESIRES

Two hours ago

soul smiles over miracles,

when we wait for mysteries,

we need hopes,

to survive till the last breath,

we tread on ropes of hope,

and dump our bodies,

in the structure of disappointments,

and glitter of silly desires,

as we drop one habit and pick up two other,

and we love,

more than...

we are loved.

SALVATION

Lions have their own share
As their purpose is ultimate
Claims to endorse get nervous attitudes
When golds shine on eyes
You are inclined to shatter
With grim countenance
With no power of insurrection
That simply grows in the mind
Can you look inside
While you trust in illusions
You can never contend with
The terrible atmosphere
On desperate injustice
You smile in the dark room
We do not need
And we never needed
Settled community
Where cosmopolitan intellectuals
Are asked to demonstrate valid efforts
To achieve the combination of racial thinking
This can be a gratuitous insult
To the history of mankind
Where you need to educate your grandfathers
And your guru admits you
Without any reward.

BACK TO SILENCE

I remember, I saw,
behind the trees,
The tender tears,
in your smiling eyes,
They meld,
beside me,
And I'll try to find,
your glancing love,
amongst the evening kisses,
with songs of birds,
drifting to the horizons,
and silence prevailed,
on sunsets,
and a culmination of fears,
in shadows,
moved like hopelessly,
uttered moans,
vanishing in the weeded journey,
of silence and indifference.
out of range of my viability.

THE PREY

I am again
to hit your alternating baits as
I burst out from the waters to breathe fresh,

you keep your smaller lures
in your weed bag
to slide my attention to your newest entice

and looking at me again out of the corner
of your eye you put your trap
on your way,

you should know aggressive
walleye inhale jigs by sucking
and can spit your lure out faster than
you can eat fresh

and this time
it is better understood as you talk
your deceptive proverb to cast
your shadows on my will

ONCE MORE

With the conscious aspect of my mind,

I can feel with my glass heart,

invisible to your crystal eyes,

and when your thin lips,

slip on the skin,

with pride in being simple,

the intricated question scrambles to the brain.

the mirror tells false,

features to myself,

being with tortures, and dragged,

and bruised, on thorns,

I scream once more,

in some nightmare.

DISAPPOINTMENTS

on wither of desire,

winds caress, my dreams,

haunting night by night,

one that stands still,

is before my eyes,

and another that,

passes with silence,

I wait for a long,

maybe a resolve of habit,

or something different,

but I am for one,

that never ends,

and never comes,

and never seen,

in disappointment.

WALLS & DOORS

your loud laughs,

wandering in the air,

like whirlwinds and clouds,

breaking the silence,

like rumbling thunders,

telling the upcoming rain,

and fears,

Prevailing over the perverted sensation

maybe I will return home,

before the falling night,

.......who is waiting for ME, I KNOW,

..................only walls & doors

A STRANGER

] When pain oozes,

from turmoil,

the flames of my desire to fire,

I know it will worsen to agony,

Present with dormant,

and volcanic strains,

Upturned from ashes,

scattered beneath,

my bare feet,

My sole blistered,

with spark,

to know at real,

that I am still a stranger,

in your eyes.

FAITH

some way,

my desires are to be blinded,

or I can wait for the inner lights,

lit in dark.

where ethics are upturned,

under a space of ruthless turmoil,

the war is undeclared,

to win is subtle and wafting in smokes,

the noises are masking,

my rancid utters,

stray life with the breath of breeze can be vital,

my heart is sun, to mind,

and certain events, when to follow,

vivid spells,

have been broken, but it is a rule,

untried feet to advance in lands of love,

and faith in THE truth.

HOMESICK

Pains make me to stay,

What I know,

Is better understood.

On the back of the walls,

There is another peril

growing in the shadows,

and hours to sharpen the loneliness

fears overrun by day,

I am homesick,

On side of the road,

the crowd passes with silence,

having candles in daylight,

and nobody is to listen to me

I MISS YOU

Walls and roof,

Of this situation...,

glow in our memories,

The swim in thoughts,

bringing sizzling lips,

to murmur,

heartfelt emotions,

to soar like surfing,

waves of deep waters,

my eyes are carpeted, on sands,

where your footsteps,

Leave imprints,

However the sunsets,

render horizons with glooms,

PAIN ENDS TO.......

While dashing over,

The cusps of my heart,

you forget,

the delicacy of rose petals,

I fear the silences of nights,

When I am driven insane in a vanished dream,

When to forget the flames of the wound?

I don't know the ends of pains,

but I know how it cuts,

and splits.

deep and bleeds,

in utters of the brain stem,

with distal radiation,

hunting in reciprocal and random.

LOOK NOW

We have left this place,

Where we used to talk, at night,

and there is now dust,

On books,

we used to hide,

rose petals in between pages,

The loneliness,

and barren walls,

are reverberating our,

spoken words,

some contact numbers,

are carved on a wooden table,

the side window is half opened,

there is whoop,

In my breaths.

There is nothing, to be back,

except we still love .

WHEN IT BECAME DIFFERENT

Words floating,

In despair on the attic surface,

spoken with the notion,

to breathe in your thoughts,

agonizing stare,

burned to ashes buried in peace,

beneath the snows,

you became different while pointing,

Your sword to me, and amazed over,

the abrupt turning,

when the earth,

Slipped from your feet.

.

WAVERING LIFE

Not just a desire,

growing from stem cells,

prone to subtle outrageous,

and contemporary consumption,

haunting politeness

with outcasts of proliferation,

infested with ill will and grudges,

and what you think, whilst growing old,

even with a prosperous life,

having little crawling kids,

and some tornado,

to ruin everything.

BORN ON A TREE

Your pleasure,

to deprive him of his liberty is counter to your silent
pride over your spasmodic laughs when you talk of,

invented tastes to sip the yolk,

and crunch of eggshells why to give

savage wolf his taste by irony to favour and disgrace to
nest with an audible whiff

of his spread wings,

a sharp breeze tickled with sparkling wines

as he learned from the sea also his vanity

to find his savory, and you shed light

in case you stunt his growth on forbidden aroma

of the soul

A DREAM OTHER THAN DREAMS

The nights create,

might and hidden, events,

and DARWEN dancing,

with monkeys,

as he was like grandpa, no,

or yes, he was,

with hairless skin, and holding,

stair shaped,

DNA helixes

arginine guanine guanine arginine guanine arginine

with a counted list of chromosomes, and genes,

and moon above his head,

all trees full of monkeys,

and I was feeling alone,

on the bank of the river.

A RAY OF HOPE

your smile

a white cloud on the sky

let the light shine in adversity

a chain of thoughts lingers

in my mind I hear your

joyful voice meeting this will become

a vital ray of hope

A STILL DESIRE

Life moves with,

every breath,

a desire stands still,

eyes seek with each blink,

the mirage keeps,

with glitters, steps are written,

on the sands,

a tale in faded words,

erasing stains her face,

love is a dream,

unforeseen unforgiven.

A SWEET SOUL

Every amorous sonnet

Cheering long hours of solitude

Having sweet memory

Of her early romantic glory

Taking her out of whispers

As the desire got wings

But like an eagle encumbered with his hood

A song fell from her lips

On strings of a mandolin

But not to deign her soul with song

Crying with various voices

With trails of tears

Like a river running its run

Moulding to eternity.

ANCIENT GRUDGES

Why you want,

to make strawberry jam

from the head of your rival,

who made you rub your nose,

on the ground,

in some business, with his,

strength of monopoly.

or you want his accident,

on the highway, and see his,

news on CNN,

while you,

take a cup of coffee.

Why you forget,

death is a universal reality,

and one day she will make,

one single delicious bite of you

while smiling over your aromatic taste,

and will wipe her lips with her tongue,

to finish your story.

APART FROM DREAMS

Dreams are volatile

and do not always stay, with me,

the contents of my vision,

are vital for my existence,

and never taken,

like the weather of yesterday.

the solace of an image,

of my person, never written,

on torn paper.

may I find it somewhere else.

AS YOU SMILE

I own your distant memories

I suffer this in moonlight

You have your fortress of sound

Since I met your nervous laugh

I am to see the dawn

Before the rest of the world

As you smile and look back.

ASYLUM

I want to hide,
From winds,
Sun and rains,
with an umbrella,
of passing time,
behind the wall,
of existence,
the life is bitter and sweet,
the death is sour and bitter,
the time is little to live,
I may carve my name,
on this wall,
some stray stranger may know me,
and tell others,
what we call asylum,
is nothing,
than trapping,
In other danger,
and silence breaks with a cry,
we must face,
what we fear to face,
and must know,
what we don't want,
to know,

ATTACHMENT

Wanted to give up,

and not to look back,

this trait of taste,

That's gone to distaste,

but hunted by smiles again.

and eyes stare with no blink,

and tongue bitten by,

rum again,

This addiction is tiring,

and I am not bad,

to kneel before,

a dream to be unfinished,

where the doors and windows,

are open to me.

all the time.

AUTUMN LEAFS

Come,

let us journey,

through the falling,

leaves of autumn,

towards the setting sun,

that enlightens,

the evening sky,

with its red glow,

come let us move,

towards our dreamscapes,

where our love shines,

in the rainbows, come let us go,

with birds, and stay,

to listen to their songs.

BENEATH THE PAIN

No more whispers no more tears

no more longing to be around

No more wreathe of fear

When I felt you lying on my side

With warmth

I saw a slowly fading voice

Like falling laughter

Dwelling beneath heavens

But loneliness whelmed

In a raging storm of seared sands

Of desert.

BEYOND DARKNESS

Facing the rage of fundamentalists

Borne with generation of lies

Might of lies stands fearless

Devouring the victories

With bloodshed brought by conspiracy theory
Hippocrates advancing toward all natural resources
Hanging corpses of rebels on poles

Why to deter their last wings

Democracy is a weapon of mass destruction

Bangs with hunger and famines

Labyrinthine beliefs about global warming

Raising their funds to grab the races.

It was fine to lie, steal and cheat,

To accomplish the bitterness of their own kind

To make you a more better person

Or you are to be killed like pests

War field overrun by Trojan Horses

The darkness lurking on new websites.

Pushing you better to stone ages

You run and hunt your own desires again

Again You watch the rage of barbarians

Slaughtering mankind with steel and fire

Again you find drifting to the bottom

Of ample arable farms and irrigable lands you lost.
Before the short-lived victories of terror.

Due to structural inequality

Lose all your sieges to survive

A life fatal to pretenders

BIG MOUTH WITCH

I am with a spell of,

some vagrant thing,

black with glowing eyes,

romping on roads,

stretching me to the thin.

magical grace,

causative of hemicrania,

ruining dollars,

a dream of Duke; she is,

my

BIG MOUTH WITCH BMW

BISCUIT BREAKER

He comes to see her,
and always with lingered hope,
and she smiles a little and turns her face,
with a deaf ear towards him,
it is all,
she keeps for him,
and more than that, he is. to become happy with.
He sits with palpitations,
and cold limbs cold sweats on his face,
He watches his fate on her face.
She is never amazed to find,
near the door when she is leaving.
And looks at him inside the mirror of her car, as he sees
her off till the car disappears from sight.,
As she goes to see her boyfriend.
She is amazing,
and he is constant,
and also more amazing,
like a teething biscuit breaker

BITTERSWEET

loving hearts leave,

but never forget,

to join again,

life is busy on her lane,

and silky touches with warmth

can make us insane,

and to cry on goodbye,

not less than any pain,

love is even bittersweet,

we need to taste this taste,

again and again,

BOUNCED VOICES

When the, returned voices,
broken into mysterious,
dark rooms,
straight from the roof of trenched,
caves telling the whispered,
realities to the timekeeper's hands,
of deliberately woven traps.
until shadowless warriors,
with their ugly swords,
moving back from safe havens,
with the curse of grimness,
overrunning the walls made,
from skulls of enemies,
of the time-honored kingdom.
and merciless taboo, roaring on sunsets.
hunting for the flower grazing, monsters.
and blood of blackbirds, and seedless plants,
burning to melt the snows,
with clearing the footprints,
of their ancestors,
leading to ended roads,
over the green valleys,
where virgins with a basket of,
flowers giggling in green and red having shower in rain
with sunshine and rainbow,
are waiting with welcome songs.

BRIGHT STARS

While I look at the sky,

on some clear night,

it looks beautiful,

I feel them talking,

in codes by flickering,

and asking me to come,

nearby them and play,

and talk with them with no fear,

and join them in purity,

and see the stardust from close.

I feel it more real when I remember,

the words of my mother,

'' I want you to be a bright star''

BRITTLE AS DESIRES

Now I see you,

not less than my desire,

wearied long before autumns,

with buried fears of quaking,

jolting my sand walls,

I wither as I know,

your veiling wishes,

I am as brittle as I was,

but still, I linger like,

dust in the air,

when caravan of my desires,

passes far in dismay,

BROKEN DREAMS

A thousand dreams shattered
Like broken forest tales
Till memories drift from the past
I sit quietly in the darkness
As the rest of the world falls apart
I refrain from the freedomless life
With parenthood of sympathies
I'll embrace the silence again
Like last standing man
With no question and no second thought
Only a quest that drags my neurons
Telling the immortal reality
Fairly preserved on the lips of the time
Feeling life pulse softly on my neck
I can still keep my head high
While I see demons in your eyes
Life will not be forsaken.
In such a dreary pattern of a dysfunctional society
And your faceless war plans
That will make you kneel in the end
Before the rogue underworlds.

BROKEN ON THE ROAD

just broken on the way,

overshadowed by acute ill-fated,

romance, defacing the skills of an artist,

bound hand the sword,

running threat for attracted,

will power portrayed in sensational,

rigors, defaced hopes, playing on,

the other sided the mirror,

standing on the foot of the tree,

listening to his glib,

devoted to the pursuit of pleasure,

remained hedonist overall,

intended to downplay,

his esoteric interests.

wanting a junket to Africa,

riding demon on his horse,

CAT EYES

this does not happen, always,

the vigilant eyes, chase shadows,

in silence, not only in dreams

but over the edge of the vested thoughts,

feeling love in shined eyes,

the fellows carve their,

heartbeats over windows.

and nights awaken,

with clicks of the clock,

and nauseous phone bell,

disturb the natural skills.

and something like powdered,

milk with essential proteins

now eyes watch something, different,

COLD WHISPER

Serenity breaks on your cold whisper
I dwell in mysteries of your echoed voice
I continue walking down with obsessions
That haunts me while longing for you
Although I can't surrender
Being loyal to what I love
Fighting the legions with an eagle's wing
For a most sacred place in my heart
Where the voice of love is born
You must not break the chain
As the end is not beginning
It is all silence in perfect time
With your wild gaze
I turn around
To forget everything
That lingers in free days
Like numbing pain of seeping cold

DARKNESS AND DAWN

When the man refused to trust
The mind enslaved in the dark ages
Needed softened light
From the dropped windowpane
To flash his real face innovation
Of power wheel
Wheedled with glittering generalities
Later turned out
With a pause at the last moments
Fueled with conservatism
Is this a funny thing about life?
Between Darkness and Dawn
Life drifted down to rest
Soft fingers caressed Man's face
And memories flooded back
Through his conscious
He accepted and owned
The reality
With all temporal blues between
Darkness and Dawn
He is prepared for every contingency.

DE NATURED

How you can go back,

to your past of mighty stories,

with rusted future,

like a person, waiting,

for someone,

who is standing at his back door.

And unkind are gazing faces at doors,

which were open day and night for you,

and draughts of hot airs,

coming to you from the monsoons clouds,

either you or everyone,

in this world is denatured.

and you want paradise,

at the price of death.

DEJECTED DESIRES

yes, my sweetheart,
I have changed my mind,
at least, ...a lot,
since the day you,
advised me,
to learn from my own madness,
and bother not to stray,
in the jungle of your wild things,
and not to use my energies,
to melt my heart and mind,
on your tears and cries,
it makes me deafened and dumb.,
ignorant, selfish, and rather indifferent.
I am not to care about,
Is anything going on anywhere else.
As I have decided, to live my own life,
whatever it may be, however,
it may be. or wherever it may be.
I may find my own ways, my own hells,
my own wills my own desires,
and I am not to bother,
thinking about your life.,
as you pushed me to, do so,
never to look back, never to look back.

DESERT LIFE

Sometimes I want to live,

the life of a desert,

with silence and indifference,

with a hiss of night winds,

changing my shapes,

my sands may settle,

sometimes with the sun,

echoes with loneliest cries,

dancing images of gigantic,

sandstorms, on my parched lips,

I may inhale the whole heat of the burning sun,

and splendid days of my love and fated hate

may deplore to die,

the rumbling cries of wind thrusts may shake

the horizons of vision.

DISORIENTATION

This day is gone,

Like other days,

what remains is uncertain,

looking back to the steps,

matters no more,

beyond that I was,

with a shadow,

now I am alone.,

Home is what,

Where I go back,

Put my shoes under,

the bed and shirt on the hanger,

close my eyes,

and open the next day,

I am the same,

the World is no more,

Like that,

DIVERGENCE

pains want me to cry,

to bring out the fears,

subduing a wrong turn,

taking a breath in suffocation

perilous trigger,

of decay,

purification on hurt,

bringing down calm,

over the hindrance,

on the pathetic,

acts of decency

DOOR OPENS

To hear the lock tumbler door opens

I want to break from reality everything vanishes

before I see what was never my notion

at last, I stood for

you walk on sick grounds

vaulted by withered stuff smokes

emerge from the cracks

your next day can smash

all you wanted

and all you never got

and you can count the crows

sitting on the wall

and exactly

we come to know

the universe is functioning perfectly

DREAMS DIE

From the chilled and cold weather
I can figure out your image
That fades out in the fogs
I fear it will be soon lost
Till the next day is over

I remember those days
When you were not out of my reach
I forget the way
We bothered to get
Out of way

If hope survives somewhere
It will grow with the moon
If it never happens
The other day is to wait
Wither miserable eyes

The lasting flame
Flutters before
It is all a smoke
And dreams die
Out of bodies

DREAMSCAPES

Like pink and white clouds,

in fluttering winds,

she waved her hands,

and smiled merrily,

after cloying talk,

her GRACE and flair eluded my mind,

there was something effervescent,

about her, some spark of mischief,

lurking in her gaze, a bright inner elan,

it was to waft away my glooms,

and sad mists,

that clung over the mountains,

of shadows, and behind that at whiles,

huge smokes to arise,

and hovered into upper winds.

EDDIES OF WIND

Havocs and whistling sounds

Thunder across my mind

My passion whirls

The rustling noise

Filling my head

I step on the cascade

And watch the brittle bones

Cursed for the abandoned pride.

I feel you are vowed

To chase my simple demise.

ENDLESS PATH

looking at other hands,

which shake for strangers,

on side roads of life.

I bore the memories,

of sweetened pains,

got on goodbyes,

from the past,

and on waiting for the future,

to spread on, like sunrise.

getting slow vigours, on defeats,

and upgraded on winning.

for me and for you, are different realities.

but the same sunshine and the moonlights.

we live and die,

for a different purpose,

let us take some road, forgetting,

generation solace, to the eternal path,

endless beverly.

EVENING SUN

Missing you on some evening
When shadows are longer
To sum up the mysteries of longing
Closing doors on sundowning
Like all the birds and flowers

Claws of cold serpentine glacier night
Inching closer and closer
Enhancing the dreams
Campaigned with zest
And love to not fall down
On yellow red and crimson
Tears of the sun

You touch gently on my shoulder
Like piano key rippling in melodious moan
your silky hair slipping
With a serene promise
To hold down hands forever

Searing Glow of the sun
Hauling your unspoken words
Cradling my nights with quiet smiles
Soothing my tender knees
Bowed on the worship of hollow wows

From nowhere a voice raised
Breaking the silence billows
With archaic sea wave
Sweeping all wows
Ruffling aimlessly on sand dunes
Of woven dreams
And I step back on night falls
On each delivered evening sun
Every time I miss you endlessly

FLAME STILL BURNS

Winds don't be so wild
I have only one candle lit in the darkness
with thrusts and splashes flutters
my violet flame while
you can take me
just with a sardonic smile
my soul goes down to native lands
you hover on top of castles on mountains
it could be so worse
and guilt lies on you with a heap of dead
leaves I close my eyes
with the faintest breath
can't see beyond whirling dust
walking on worn stone steps
dragging down to dimness
I can find my destiny.

FLOWERS AND MEMORIES

If my earnest desire no longer whispers

timely utterance echoed through mountain

throng my words might reach you

like silent raindrops from the depth of silence

let it melt the iceand bloom

the feeble pointed spikes of flowers in blowing

winds if you find rose petals

in your way

my love that laid swale in rows

FOCUSED SOULS

tampered love,

sizzling soul,

keeping alive,

by burning bones,

turning in smokes,

recalculating,

reciprocal breaths,

the sound of a clock,

on the dusty wall,

beating heart,

counting days,

happy ones,

ringing bells,

ringing bells,

dancing girl,

dancing girl,

ending in well.

FOG MOON

I hold you in my heart

As I dream in my sleep

You never know

How it comes back

Like a moon

Which vanished in a tender fog

Standing on the toes

My hope longs for a caress

From the breeze

Which flickers like a smile

On your lips

FORGIVENESS

forgive me
for my broken heart
my parched lips
and my dusty hair

I plunged down to a descend
like the evening sun
and there was no one to listen
in the desert my last scream

your cry for your broken dreams
raised in intensification barren
flushing of suffered deprivations
as I gave up my courage on every search
of my wayward surveillance of ruthless time

it becomes spread of invisible immerse of broken
promises round hollows before my eyes
as time gets closer to a pause

I suppose
my endearing
voice can cross horizons and all limits
that prevail
in between you and me

FREEDOM OF SOUL

My utter becomes unkind

wilderness awakens from the silence

it will be a furtive glimpse of his beast

will I adore my wish

my honor to soar in the moonlight

I shackle my desire again

if I could not love you anymore

it will be a hangover in my life or as I adore

sovereign soul to be freed

from the castles of abandoned pride

FROM MOON WITH LOVE

Green blue and bright,

come down my sweet Earth,

the moon is no more barren,

it comes from you,

and like a candle, in the sky,

love glows in the nights,

where life is to grow,

and sparrows flutter in air,

and mists over the green,

and clouds over the sea,

bring me all with you,

I am here on the moon,

you are there on the earth,

GOOD NIGHT FRIENDS

A glimpse of delight pride of serenity

the jubilant gaze of sublime seashore splendid attire

with ripples of smile and myriad blessings

you are a melody in memories

Even I adore such a brighter day

Sun falls down in the lap of horizon

Fugitive shadows lay down

After losing a long battle

Souls bereft of their loves

surrounded by garish white walls

Of ornate tombs

With voiceless cries,

my nightmare was like

A drum that sounds without being touched

I walked down the ladder

Dragged the iron door

And locked it

Goodnight friends.

GOODNIGHT DREAMS

my dreams are alive,

with the rhythm of life,

the vistas they have seen,

for all long my life,

the dream fill my nights,

with fantasies of life,

my eyes want to see,

what my brain dreamed,

like a winged fairy,

that can fly,

with bunches of flowers,

from earth to heavens,

and shaking me out,

from my deepen sleeps,

I want to have, such dreams,

after every goodnight.

GRATITUDE

All of suddenness,

waves strike the shore,

we miss the moments,

that endow the gratitude

for every solemn sunrise,

and the rest of the world falls apart.

Diamonds of memories swirl

on every wave crest

as waves tumble them onward

with distant vision and such a sunrise is seldom seen.

We find the aroma of gratitude,

When the world is astounded hearing such words.

It is infinite, for which we hunger

and we ride gladly on every little wave.

If we are to fall, we must fall now,

as the sky sphere is mounting the

Earth sphere with such palpable happier moments

.If even the whole world is be blazed,

we ourselves should be consigned to eternity.

We boast and differ from winds, waves,

and falling stones.

GRIEVOUS INJUSTICES

You smiled coldly
To blow dust from an old book of memories
Like the action of winds
Thrusting through desert of stunted trees
Until disaster strikes the shores
we all fall apart as drifting leaves
As aspirants making solemn vows
Through silent yards
Listening to the music moans
Suffered from the weariness of awakening eyes
Dazzled by sudden sunlight.
Feeling alone in solace and panics
Of antenatal life with pre-eclampsia
When life begins filling the holly dreams with fears
Built upon the shores of heavens.
Our souls were banished to the earth with survivals
we have to prove ourselves
As only cold-blooded creatures
who can face the torture
Of grievous injustices

HALLUCINATING SPACES

Fallen down from,

breathless ascend,

my passions dispelled in winds,

blood dripping on grass blades,

beast seeking my taste,

Pains ended in euphoria,

While aching jolts,

shaking my worth,

ruthless vultures,

scrabbling over my flesh,

my soul crying for help.

HAPPY GIRL'S DAY

Happy girls day

It looks beautiful

Solidarity and compassion

And the world begins

A journey that never ends

Foundation of wisdom

And education cement

The generations

Our beacons of light shine

Every girl when born

Our morale as a nation Rises

HARD TIMES

Your wrapped but perfidious smiles,

haunt me,

like strikes of ironic fate,

while I am walking through,

a crowd with my absent mind.

Murmuring the bitter song of,

your loud laughs.

And I see my desire pinned on street walls,

While the worn outdoors,

and windows opened,

and graced with gazing eyes.

like birds sitting on trees,

wanting to rest after sunset.

with the night is studded with unkind treachery,

on the way, paved with cobblestones and trash.

HARVESTED DAWN

sleeping with and,

onside of night,

and spreading prevailed,

loneliness,

up to farsighted futures,

waiting for someone,

coming down from,

milky ways of stardust,

and another star to break up,

one astray asteroid to blind me,

and likely to hope for,

another missed fortune,

on my frothier lips,

with murmur of another whispered wild cry.

and pain awakening from,

breed of nightmarish sleep.

and the sky is not far from my one arm length,

becoming domed,

covering above all, my thoughts

with harvested memories.

I am to wait for the upcoming dawn,

HEALING

on some, other days,

you will know,

and you will say,

in some,

different way, that,

the inner,

is somewhat different,

than the outer,

it is chaotic from, inside,

and also healing,

of wounds,

is not from out iside,

the dressing is to do, a little,

healing comes,

always from inside.

HEAVENLY BLISS

Look at the bird

On your side

And wave crests

Thrusts of wind soaring

Within the haze of the horizons

And curl of your raven hair winding around

The pensive gaze in daring thrill

With divinity

The chirp of the bird

Unleashed his soul around

With the prism of your rainbow

Rush like a sea wave

To embrace the heavenly bliss

HER FEUDAL LORD

Her pleasure dances with his shadows she dwells

with her feudal lord in her daydreams moving with

his evasive derivation of capitalism

her surreal dreams grow with his gun powders she
quenches

her sensations

in caressing his baldness she never forgets

the aroma of his perspiration while

he stages the stories of his tiger hunt.

HOPEFUL

it may be attention or tired gesture,

to swim in swamped tragedies,

rather an unfaith,

or divided mindful,

ravel in stubbornness,

even in understanding,

troubled from inner,

but the mountains of,

success is never under feet,

The tolerance is last to suffer,

eyes wait for changes,

from dark to dawn,

and hopes,

are harvested fates.

that breath in the heavens.

HOW STRANGE IT IS

when we were to fear winds,

like autumn leaves,

when we were to elope,

in our hidden dreams,

when we were to awaken,

together on chilled nights,

and cry with sore eyes,

with broken hopes,

and straying in swamps of dismay,

with orchids hearts,

and we were to paint,

our love hillock gaily,

with our green visions,

it was spade of mine,

and a dream of yours,

and now how strange it is,

that you don't know me.

HOW YOU CAN FORGET ME

something,
something which,
is breaking my soul,
I want to know,
how it happens,
how you can forget my dreams,
how you are to leave me,
with my bleeding soul this way,
I see from the window,
sadly branches of autumn,
approaching my hands
from broken rays of moonlight,
and wishes of winds,
gathering withered leaves,
and blowing pieces of ice,
on my face,
my freezing lips, murmur the sorrows,
I see the slow moon,
in front of my eyes,
some round circles of gloom,
and crystallized rays,
fallen on my face,
a row of tears,
frozen on my face,
I am never in me,
always waiting, the time,
you touch my soul, always in dreams,

which are never mine, I am raising my arms,
to hold you in my thoughts, it is no more like that,
it is sinking since my, will is feeble,
over tides of frothing waves,
my feet are swollen,
I see fire, and my dreams,
and remains of impalpable ashes and blue sky,
sinking in his doom,
and stars are no more,
shine of my eyes,
I am unable to see,
things before me,
a faded image of tears,
I want to know,
who was that,
if it was not you,
to hold me,
in the lap of seashore,
a promised paradise,
and the steps on the sands,
Waterbeach so sad,
waves ran over my

I AM AWAKE YOU ARE IN MY EYES

my sweet,
my heart,
my soul
I was to wait,
for you for long with my eyes,
staring, always, the ways for,
you, until, you, are hereby,
near me soothing my eyes,
touching my soul,
you are brightness,
of my home,
the desire of my, heart,
I love to sleep with you,
and wake up with you,
have, breakfast, with you,
when I am ready,
for my office, you,
take me in your arms,
and smile, like rose,
see me from the door,
till I move for office,
and keep on waiting,
till I am back, home,
I love you, my soul,
with a promise,
to never say,
goodbye.

ABOUT THE AUTHOR

RAFIQUE FAROOQI

Date of birth: 22 April 1959

I was born in dist. Gujranwala Pakistan, I matriculated from govt. High School Qilla Didar Singh, FSc from Government College, Lahore, and MBBS from Allama Iqbal Medical College Lahor, in 1984, I am doing my G.P practices, at Lahore, Writing is my Hobby.